Child's Guide
to the Beatitudes

By Kathy DellaTorre O'Keefe

Illustrations by Anne Catharine Blake

Paulist Press
New York / Mahwah, NJ

To Dr. David Butler, M.D., and all those who responded
to Jesus' words in the Beatitudes, reaching out
to assist the earthquake victims of Haiti.
KDTO

For little Obed Henry Otto
ACB

The scripture quotations contained herein are from the *New Revised Standard Version Bible: Catholic Edition*, Copyright © 1989, 1993 National Council of the Churches of Christ in the U.S.A. Used by permission. All rights reserved.

Library of Congress Cataloging-in-Publication Data

O'Keefe, Kathy DellaTorre.
  Child's guide to the Beatitudes / written by Kathy DellaTorre O'Keefe ; illustrated by Anne Catharine Blake.
    p. cm.
  ISBN 978-0-8091-6756-2 (alk. paper)
  1. Beatitudes--Juvenile literature. 2. Catholic children--Religious life--Juvenile literature. I. Blake, Anne Catharine. II. Title.
  BT382.O54 2011
  241.5'3--dc22
                    2010041064
Published by Paulist Press
997 Macarthur Boulevard
Mahwah, New Jersey 07430

www.paulistpress.com

Printed and bound in Shenzhen, China
by Shenzhen Donnelley Printing Co. Ltd.
February 2011

Hi, my name is Juan Carlos. I'm glad you came to school today.

There's Father Mike. He's preparing today's religion lesson on the **Beatitudes**.

The word *Beatitude* means "blessings." God is always blessing us, every moment of every day, with his love and guidance. He is a special part of our lives!

A very long time ago, Jesus gathered with a group of people like us. They were moms, dads, grandparents, and children who wanted to learn more about God.

This was an important occasion. It's called the **Sermon on the Mount** because Jesus climbed up a hill in order to speak to the people.

Jesus knew there were people in the crowd who were sad and tired, and who had a lot of problems. He wanted them to know that God was always blessing them and giving them the strength to deal with their problems.

These special blessings are called the **Eight Beatitudes**. The story of the Beatitudes is told in Matthew's Gospel. Matthew was a friend of Jesus and one of the apostles. He was probably there when Jesus was teaching the crowd.

Can you find Jesus in the crowd?

Let's go into class and learn more about the Beatitudes. Here, sit next to me.

"The First Beatitude is, '*Blessed are the poor in spirit, for theirs is the kingdom of heaven,*'" says Father Mike. "*The poor in spirit* are people who are not filled with pride. They know that if they are open to God's grace, they will lead good and happy lives. Even if they are sick or sad, or are facing difficult problems, God is with them and is helping them."

"Jesus understood what it meant to feel poor in spirit because he knew his friends would let him down, and he would feel great pain at the end of his life. He did not avoid dying on the cross but trusted that God would provide the strength he needed and would always be with him."

"Isaiah, please read the Second Beatitude."

"'*Blessed are those who mourn, for they will be comforted.*' What does *mourn* mean, Father Mike?"

"To mourn means to feel really sad. We mourn when someone we love has died. And, we must remember that love is a gift from God. If we had not received that gift, we would not be mourning or really sad that someone we love had died."

"Jesus wanted the crowd to know that God understands our suffering and our pain. He also wanted them to understand that God comforts us because he loves us. Jesus can use you and me to comfort others who are mourning."

"My friend Hilda was very sad because her grandmother died," says Jasmine. "I hugged her really tight. I wanted her to feel better and think of how happy her grandmother must be with God in heaven. I would cry for days if my grandmother died. I love her so much."

How can you comfort someone who is sad? What would you say to them?

"Jasmine, please read the Third Beatitude."

"'*Blessed are the meek, for they will inherit the earth.*'"

"Someone who is *meek* does not get angry or try to get even when someone hurts them," Father Mike explains. "Jesus was meek because he didn't waste his life hating people—even those who hurt him. Instead, Jesus chose to love those who hated him."

"But a meek person is not a weak person. He or she is someone who wants to serve God and others and doesn't brag about it.

"Jesus tells us the story of the Pharisee and the tax collector. The Pharisee thinks he is a wonderful person because he doesn't sin like his neighbors. The tax collector admits his sins and praises God (Luke 18:9–14). Who is the meek person in this story?" asks Father Mike.

"The tax collector!" shouts Judy.

"That's right," Father Mike says. "Jesus tells us the meek person is the one most pleasing to God."

"Would you like to tell us the Fourth Beatitude, Judy?"

"'*Blessed are those who hunger and thirst for righteousness, for they will be filled.*'"

"*Righteousness* means to listen to what God is telling us and do what is right," explains Father Mike. "Jesus knows making the right choice can be hard. But, knowing that God is always there to help us is a wonderful blessing from him."

"Mother Teresa believed God wanted her to do what was right by helping *the poorest of the poor*. She started communities to help the poor and sick in Calcutta, India, and around the world. She inspired others to help those in need, too! Through her daily prayer, the Rosary, and Communion, God blessed Mother Teresa with her special gift for always helping the poor, the sick, and those in greatest need."

"Yes, Mother Teresa made the right choice. But, sometimes we make the wrong choices," Father Mike says. "We are unkind to our friends, our classmates, and even our families. We act like bullies through our mean words and actions, hurting each other, and hurting God, too."

"Juan Carlos, why is your head down?"

"Yesterday, I acted like a bully. I hurt my friend Kevin. I called him names. I made him cry and run away. Now, I'd like to tell him I'm sorry."

"Saying you're sorry is the right choice, Juan Carlos. It will make you feel better to do what is right. That's what it means to be filled or satisfied."

**Have you ever been a bully? Did you tell them you were sorry?
Has someone ever bullied you? How did you feel?**

"Joseph, what's the Fifth Beatitude?"

"'*Blessed are the merciful, for they will receive mercy.*'"

"Jesus knows that every human being needs *mercy*. Every one of us has hurt others. And, every one of us has been hurt by others."

"To understand what mercy means, we have to remember what Jesus says in the Lord's Prayer: '*Forgive us our trespasses as we forgive those who trespass against us.*' God freely gives mercy and forgives us for any wrong that we do. And, he asks that we do the same, by giving mercy and forgiveness to those who hurt us."

"I forgave my brother when he broke my bike," says David.

"I'm sure that was very hard to do and very pleasing to God," replies Father Mike.

Do you forgive others when they hurt you?
Do you think it's hard to be merciful?

"David, please read the Sixth Beatitude."

"'*Blessed are the pure in heart, for they will see God.*'"

"When we are *pure of heart*, we place God above all things. Friends, family, money, and education are all important things, but they are not more important than God. That means it is important to love and honor God."

"We honor God by loving others, by forgiving them, and by helping them when they are in need. It is most important for us, as Catholics, to honor God by regularly attending Mass and receiving the Body and Blood of Jesus in Holy Communion," Father Mike says.

"As Christians, we are asked to put God before everything else. Those who put God first serve him by helping others in many, many ways. And so, millions of people all over the world have come to know Jesus because of the pure of heart," says Father Mike.

"Saint Augustine didn't always put God first. Sometimes, he made bad choices. But, through God's grace, Augustine became pure of heart and put God first in his thoughts and actions. He became a priest and then a bishop, and did many good things. He believed that our hearts are restless until they rest in God."

Do you put God first in your life?
Do you feel God's presence in your family, friends, and the things you do? How?

"We have two more Beatitudes left. Robert, can you read the seventh?"

"'*Blessed are the peacemakers, for they will be called children of God.*'"

Father Mike explains that a peacemaker is someone who brings peace and love where there is anger and hatred.

"Class, who was the greatest peacemaker that ever lived?"

"Jesus!" shouts Juan Carlos.

"Yes! That's why we call him the Prince of Peace," says Father Mike. "The first time Jesus visited his apostles after his death, he greeted them with the words: 'Peace be with you.' These are the same words we say to our family and friends during Mass."

"Peacemakers can be kings, presidents, or people like you and me. A peacemaker is anyone who imitates Jesus and spreads kindness and love to one person, a group of people, or even the world.

"That means you can be a peacemaker simply by choosing not to argue or fight with your family or friends. Anyone can fight, but Jesus said that peacemakers are specially blessed by God."

Can you find the peacemakers in the pictures?

"Now let's read the Eighth Beatitude together:

"'*Blessed are those who are persecuted for righteousness' sake, for theirs is the kingdom of heaven.*'

"This Beatitude encourages us to obey God's Word and to do what is right, even when it's hard to do because people don't agree with us," says Father Mike.

"We are given the strength we need to live our Catholic faith and share it through the awesome power of the Holy Spirit. We receive the Spirit at our baptism and the Spirit is strengthened in us through the sacrament of confirmation," says Father Mike. "We believe it is right to share our faith and to be eager to spread God's Word."

"Ever since the first Pentecost, people who love and follow Jesus have spread his Word to millions of people around the world. Some, like Saint Peter, became martyrs when they died for their faith. Each one of them believed that true life is found in following Jesus. So, we can live a true life by following Jesus."

These are the Eight Beatitudes—the blessings from God that draw us closer to him even when we suffer.

The Beatitudes are a sign of God's great love for us. The Beatitudes bring us closer to Jesus and to God, the Father. They lead us on a path to true life, which begins on earth and lasts forever.

Will you welcome God's blessings and follow the path of the Beatitudes? God is counting on you to say YES!

FOR FURTHER DISCUSSION

Scripture tells us that Jesus ended his Sermon on the Mount by saying, "Blessed are you when people revile you and persecute you and utter all kinds of evil against you falsely on my account. Rejoice and be glad, for your reward is great in heaven" (Matt 5:11–12).

1) Do you think Jesus knows that sometimes we feel sad and hurt and we are unhappy?
2) Do you think it's hard or easy to follow Jesus? Why?
3) Why do you think some people choose not to follow Jesus?
4) When we talk about going to Mass and Holy Communion regularly, do you think this is something we should do? Why?
5) Why does Jesus want us to tell people about him?
6) If you are rejoicing and glad, do you think you'll feel happy?
7) Jesus says your reward will be great in heaven. What do you think heaven will be like?